AF527667

DATING & MARRIAGE DIARIES IN URBAN INDIA

A No-Nonsense Guide to Finding your Perfect Partner

notionpress.com

DATING & MARRIAGE
DIARIES IN URBAN INDIA

A No-Nonsense Guide to Finding your Perfect Partner

SAHIL THAKER

notionpress.com

Notion Press

Old No. 38, New No. 6

McNichols Road, Chetpet

Chennai - 600 031

First Published by Notion Press 2015

Copyright © Sahil Thaker 2015

All Rights Reserved.

ISBN: 978-93-52062-44-7

This book has been published in good faith that the work of the author is original. All efforts have been taken to make the material error-free. However, the author and the publisher disclaim the responsibility.

No part of this book may be used, reproduced in any manner whatsoever without written permission from the author, except in the case of brief quotations embodied in critical articles and reviews.

Legal Disclaimer

The information presented in this book represents the views of the author as of the date of publication. This book is for informational and awareness purposes only. *This book does not aim to offend any religion, caste or persons. While the situations described in the book are real, no real names have been used in order to protect the privacy of the people involved.*

While every attempt has been made to verify the information in this book, neither the author nor the publisher assumes any responsibility for errors, inaccuracies or omissions. Neither the publisher nor the individual author shall be liable for any physical, psychological, emotional, financial, or commercial damages, including, but not limited to, special, incidental, consequential or other damages. You are responsible for your own choices, actions, and results. Any legal dispute is subject to Mumbai jurisdiction only.

Preface

Marriage is probably the single most important decision people will make in their adult life. The implications of marriage are often profound and life changing. A good spouse can fill your life with happiness and love whereas a bad spouse can make your life a living hell. The mental, emotional and financial costs of a marriage gone wrong can be staggering. This hard hitting and well researched book aims to show the cold reality of finding a spouse in Urban India, and not the type of romance that is so commonly portrayed in novels or Bollywood movies.

If you are a parent of a son or daughter who is of marriageable age then you will have justifiable concerns regarding selecting a good spouse for your child. This book should help you to make more informed and better decisions. This book provides valuable tips to keep you safe, avoid bad situations, make the journey of finding your spouse enjoyable, and hopefully have a strong, happy and lasting marriage.

This must read book is written in a simple, easy to read and understand way for a wide audience. I believe the success of this book will be decided by how many lives this book can touch in a positive way, and by how many people feel benefited from reading this book.

For many foreigners, India remains a land of contradictions and mystery. Dating and marriage in India is inherently more complex compared to most other countries around the world. For non-Indian readers, this book offers a fascinating insight into how the urban Indian society works when it comes to dating and marriage.

Contents

The History of Dating and Marriage In India

Dating is a word which is relatively new to India. Historically and especially in the absence of internet, dating (or the absence of it) used to be a fairly straight forward affair. Parents, relatives, extended family, *panditji (priest)* etc. would look for prospective brides and grooms in the community and introduce the two families. Once horoscope would match the *arranged marriage* would be fixed. The guy and the girl would probably be given less than an hour to talk and decide if they wanted to marry or not. In many cases they would just say yes if their parents told them to.

Fast forward to modern urban India. The entire dynamics have changed. Extended and joint families have become a minority. Most people in urban India aged under 30 either have just one sibling or none. Women have become a lot more independent, educated and working at well-paying jobs. Yet it has become increasingly difficult for young people to find suitable spouses. You might be working in the same office but in different departments with no chances of even meeting each other.

Proliferation of online dating sites can open huge new possibilities for meeting people whom you would have never otherwise met. You are able to narrow down your searches based on every imaginable parameter such as height, income, complexion, religion, caste and even sub caste! You can be a guy sitting in Pune and still be able to connect with a beautiful girl in Bangalore. In normal situations you would have never even met this girl, let alone be able to talk to her.

Since I have lived in Mumbai only all of my life and in the USA for about six years, I have zero idea about how finding a spouse works in rural and semi urban parts of India. Over the years, I used to keep a handwritten diary of my interactions with various girls as I was looking for a spouse. Inspiration struck and I decided to write this book. Hence the title of this book "Dating and Marriage Diaries in Urban India".

The Types of Girls You Will Meet Online

Online matrimonial sites expose you to a large number and types of girls whom you would not have met otherwise through usual channels. The usual channels I am referring to are family, friends, co-workers and college/university. It has been overwhelming at times but nevertheless an interesting experience. While it is impossible for me to cover every single type of girl you will ever meet, I have tried to group them into types which I most commonly came across.

I personally do not judge any of these girls but just lay the true facts before you, the reader of this book. You are free to draw your own conclusions.

The Ugly

I am not just referring to physical beauty (although that is a part of it too). This type of girl usually has the following characteristics.

- She is almost always overweight or obese.
- Has no sense of dress. Her photos usually make you feel as if you should just stay single for the rest of your life rather than even think about her.
- Her hair is uncombed or in a bad shape.
- None of her photos show her smiling, happy or cheerful.
- The profile is incomplete with absolutely no sentences regarding themselves, what their background is, what their expectations are etc.
- The sentences (if any) are full of spelling mistakes with no proper grammar.

I admit some obesity might be due to genetic or other factors but such cases are very rare. Most obesity is caused only due to lack of regular exercise and unhealthy diet. Women do gain weight with age and during pregnancy and I have no problems with that. I feel that 20 something women (and men too!) must be in the best shape of their lives.

Most people simply fail to grasp the serious long term effects of excess weight. Overweight and obesity can cause or exacerbate pre-existing conditions such as high blood pressure, heart diseases and diabetes. Women can also have additional risks of osteoporosis and osteoarthritis because of excess weight and poor diet.

If you are overweight or obese the chances of having overweight or obese children is increased significantly. Childhood obesity has become a serious public health issue in the United States of America. China (which has a one child policy) has also seen a big rise in childhood obesity. The only children of their parents who are called "little emperor" or "little empress" tend to be quite overweight or obese.[1] One can only imagine what will be the health of these children a few years down the road unless some serious corrective action is taken soon.

Key tip: Girls (and guys too!) should have a smiling and pleasing personality. It is important to invest in your own health and fitness.

The VISA Queen

No, I am not talking about the VISA credit or debit card, but about girls who sole ambition in life is to find a guy who is living in USA, Canada, Australia or UK. She has scant interest in you, but tries to be with you so that she can get that coveted green card or permanent residency.

I myself had a rather bad experience with such a girl. Barely a month after I had returned from USA, I received an interest from a tall, good looking Gujarati Brahmin girl living in Ahmedabad. We chatted a bit online and after a few days exchanged phone numbers. I could see myself liking her as she sounded very nice and caring until she showed her true colors. After a couple of weeks, she asked me on the phone when I planned to go back to the US. (I had clearly mentioned on my profile that I had relocated to Mumbai and was planning to stay here.) I was a bit surprised and informed her that I had no desire to go back after living there for so long. Her tone changed immediately and she asked why I was wasting her time. She further said that she had expressed an interest in me hoping that I would be taking her to USA pretty soon.

The girl in question was only a B.A and had no skills or work experience at all. Yet she was expecting someone would just marry her in a few weeks and take her to USA so that she can live comfortably for the rest of her life. If she indeed wished to immigrate there, then she should have gotten a good education, tried to get a job there and live there. Instead she had chosen an easy way out.

When girls behave in such a way, they knowingly or unknowingly make themselves vulnerable to NRI guys (not all NRIs are like this, but a substantial number are) who marry such girls in sham marriages and then just disappear. The trick guys use is simple. They would be making $8 an hour (which is about the minimum wage in USA) washing dishes at a restaurant. Before coming to India they go on a shopping spree buying cheap but good looking clothes, shoes, perfumes, sunglasses at discount stores in USA to impress such gullible girls and their families. This helps them create an impression that they are living like millionaires there.

Other tricks include clicking your photo next to a random luxury car in the parking lot and then claiming that you own it. Once in India the marriages are quickly fixed and the girl's family always ends up paying a fat dowry so that their daughter will have a "bright future" abroad.

Such marriages almost always end in divorces, and the girls and their families are left holding the bag. In the worst case scenario, they even have a child with the father of the child having long disappeared. If you do not believe me do a little research online and you will find tens of thousands of such cases.

Key tip: Marrying someone living abroad carries substantial risk even in the best of times. If you choose to go down this path, then be extra careful and do it at your own risk.

The Princess

The single most important thing about such a girl is her (actually her parents') wealth. You can spot a girl like this from a mile away. She usually has expensive designer clothes, purses, handbags and shoes (lots of them!).

I have had quite a misfortune dealing with a few princesses first hand. A popular matrimonial site in India offers "VIP" service for those willing to spend. Parents of these princesses are willing to pay a fortune to find the best possible grooms for their offspring. An agent hired by mom and dad usually approaches me to see if I am interested in the daughter. The trouble is that their daughter is least interested in marriage or any sort of commitment as it will seriously infringe on their active social life and profligate shopping habits.

I was approached by such an agent during mid 2014 for an affluent Indore based family for their youngest daughter. This was the first time ever I had even heard of such a service. After exchanging a couple of emails with her dad, I was given the contact details of his daughter. The daughter was average looking, but at that time I didn't have any other prospects lined up, so I decided to take a chance and see how things went. Soon I would realize what a mistake I had made. First of all, the girl was living and working in Ahmedabad and there appeared to be communication issues between the dad and daughter. When I first contacted her, she was totally surprised as to who I was, which was very strange given the fact that it was her family who had approached me and that too through a VIP marriage agent!

From then on, things just went from bad to worse. She appeared to be heavily into strange artistic things and was a social justice warrior. I am scientific, logical and rational in my approach. Our phone and online conversations often ended in bitter arguments. In just one week, I had enough of her. In a final phone conversation with her dad, he did say I was a good guy and it was disappointing that things could not go further.

The dad genuinely appeared to be a kind of person that I would love to have as father-in-law, but the daughter was more or less completely out of his control. Parents of such girls somehow feel that finding a nice guy will automatically change their daughter for the better. *Raising kids well is the job of parents, and not future spouses!*

Looking back, I feel glad that I was over it fairly quickly, rather than dragging on for months. While many guys would be tempted to marry into a rich family no matter what, I am not among them.

Key tip: Never marry for money. It's very rare to find a girl who is rich and is level headed.

The Over-Enthusiastic Parent/Relative/ Sibling

This type is not really the girl but her entire extended family which can include parents, maternal and paternal uncles and aunties, siblings and sometimes even friends. The biggest trouble with someone else making and handling your profile is that they will use their expectations while looking for a spouse for you. Some people think that since family elders are more experienced, younger people should listen to them. The fact is, you might consult them before deciding on marriage and take their advice, but ultimately it's your life, and it's you who have to marry and live with that person.

Some of the problems observed while dealing with such types are:

Obsession with horoscope matching

Indian parents for some reason are obsessed with matching horoscopes before even talking and getting to know you. They firmly believe that if horoscopes match, then the married couple will have a happy future together. Just visit a family court in your city and ask any couple undergoing divorce if they had their horoscope matched before their marriage.

In today's world there is absolutely no guarantee that you will be even alive tomorrow, let alone predict your married life for the next 30 or 40 years!

Package

Parents of most girls these days absolutely demand that the guy must have a lucrative job. From my observation it seems the minimum package a guy must have is 15 lacs per annum. On paper it sounds good, that having more income or money automatically means a happy life. But people here have not seen US style capitalism in which even the best paid and most experienced people can be laid off at a moment's notice. Please watch the Hollywood movie *"The Company Men"* to get an idea regarding what I am talking about. I have devoted an entire section to this later in the book.

Absentee photos

This is one my pet peeves and this non-sense repeats itself almost on a daily basis. Profiles with no photos used to keep hitting on me almost every day.

I have had very impressive sounding profiles which have read something like this

"My daughter is very good looking, fair, slim and well educated. She has been a topper throughout and was first in her college. Currently she is working in an MNC with a package of 10 lakhs per annum."

"We are an affluent business family looking for a perfect groom for our perfect daughter. She is very beautiful, smiling and affectionate. Her hobbies include cooking, dancing, singing and knitting."

In rare cases when I actually get photos by email, I immediately realize why these photos were not posted on the website. The simple reason is that these girls tend to be ugly and nowhere even close to what their impressive sounding profiles suggest.

Wanting to talk to my parents immediately

I have been born and brought up in a fairly liberal family and right from an early age was free to make all my decisions for myself. However only recently have I begun to realize how orthodox and conservative many families are.

I have had such orthodox parents of girls contact me the moment I accepted their interest or they accepted mine, and they would demand (not even ask) that they immediately talk to my parents. My parents and I found this very annoying, as we felt the girl and the guy should at least chat online and talk a bit on the phone before parents get involved. If the talks on phone go well, then the parents may choose to get involved.

Terrible grammar

This is more or less self-explanatory. Below is just one example in case you were thinking that I am bluffing. This is an exact profile that had expressed interest in me.

"She is my signal daughter. She want small, educated, welset family. Western line only till borivali. Very Loving & caring person she want."

Key tip: The girl should be actively involved in the selection process and not parents or relatives.

Awaiting Divorce or Divorced

In the past decade or so the number of divorces in Tier 1 cities in India has gone up significantly. Tier 2 and Tier 3 cities are not far behind either. Marriage and divorce are probably two of the biggest decisions people make in their lifetime.

I don't even remember the number of times girls who were just 22 or 23 and were already divorced or awaiting divorce hit on me. It sounded very abnormal so as to why someone would marry at such a young age, and if they indeed got married what could have been the reasons for divorce.

The worse types of girls (or their parents) are those who already start contacting guys even though their divorce is not even finalized yet! The ink on the divorce paperwork is not even dry yet, and they want to get married again. It sounds very creepy to me.

Once, a 23 year old divorced girl from Gandhinagar had expressed interest in me. For the sake of curiosity, I decided to accept her interest and chat with her to know more about her situation. Upon asking the reasons for marriage and subsequent divorce at such a young age, she told me her story.

She said her marriage was fixed by the parents only a couple of years ago, to an NRI guy in USA. She had ambitions to go abroad, and accepted it immediately without even getting to know the guy much. Since parents were involved, they met only a couple of times before the marriage. Upon going to USA she found out that her husband was not even employed at a proper job, and that he was having an affair with his Bhabhi (sister in law)! She went through a bad time and returned to India within 6 months of her marriage. Then they got divorced. She seemed very bitter and resentful about the whole situation. While I felt sorry for her, her case had resemblance to the VISA queen as described previously. I did wish her good luck in her search and that was the end of it.

Many women, who are divorced or are currently undergoing divorce, often have serious emotional issues which can be very difficult to deal with. These days most people have enough problems of their own, and dealing with such a girl is only likely to increase those problems.

Key tip: If you want to date/marry a divorcee then my advice is to wait at least 6 months to a year *after* the divorce has been legally granted. This may give them enough time to put their life back on track.

The Over-Liberated

This girl is the life of every party. While liberation of women from a traditional patriarchal society may be a good thing, there are also several downsides to the same. Some of these downsides are smoking, excessive consumption of alcohol, taking recreational drugs, and entering into casual relationships. Some of these things are elaborated later in the book.

I am by no means a conservative or narrow minded guy. My own mother has been working full time at a bank even before I was born. I do support women's right to work if they choose to and be free. But the choices you make should be good and wise.

Economic growth in India is fairly recent compared to developed countries. My years of living in the US managed to give me a rare insight into how people and societies evolve over an extended period of time. The source of power of these types of girls comes from the fact that they happen to have a good paying job. Once you start making money you can supposedly live in your own apartment (in most cases far from the eyes of your parents and extended family), be able to enjoy the nightlife in your city, drink, smoke, travel and do lots of shopping. Thanks to easy availability of credit cards and EMI, a whole lifestyle of 'consume a lot now and pay later' has developed.

During the economic booms of the 1990s and early 2000s in USA, many women working in well paid but high pressure jobs in finance, banking, media and public relations gave up their years in the 20s and early 30s chasing freedoms (living on your own + car), booze, and getting in and out of relationships.

Fast forward to the present day. The lucrative high paying job for which they were ready to sell their soul to the devil is probably no longer there. During the economic meltdown during late 2000s hundreds of thousands of jobs just disappeared along with dozens of large corporations. Many of these women (and men too) are now in their 40s, divorced, either with or without kids. I personally happened to know a couple of well educated women in their 40s, who regretted not having kids while they still could.

While this sounds farfetched for India, things such as rising divorce rates and single parent families are already increasing in urban India.

Key tip: Freedom and responsibility go hand in hand. If you abuse your freedom and make poor choices then you alone should bear the responsibility for the same.

The Hardworking Types

Just until a couple of decades ago, most women used to be housewives. As times have changed more and more women increasingly have to juggle both home and career responsibilities properly. I happened to come across a few such hardworking types. Such types aren't easy to find. Below is the story of my interaction with a hardworking girl.

In September 2014 I happened to get in touch with a girl based in Pune. She was a trained classical dancer and also a part time model. Over a period of a few weeks, we started chatting online and by phone and I started to get to know her better. Her day used to begin like this. She woke up early every morning and hit the gym around 6.30 AM. After spending over an hour working out, she used to head home and get ready for her dancing practice. She later explained it to me that working out was important for her because dancing and modelling both demanded that she be in top shape. Almost every day she spent a few hours with her teacher training, and then also taught her students. She was also a part of a theatre group with whom she had to perform various stage shows. For these shows she had to travel across India and occasionally abroad.

At the same time she being the only child of her parents, also had household responsibilities. Since her dad was not well, she once drove her car hundreds of kilometers across Maharashtra to take her mom to various far off temples they usually go to each year. I was definitely impressed with this girl who was not only hard-working but a dutiful daughter to her parents too. Many parents in India who think girls are a liability should look up to daughters like her.

Ultimately her hectic and erratic schedule and not being based in Mumbai took a toll, and we realized it was difficult to take things forward.

Key tip: Working hard is a good thing but at the same time you should relax and do fun activities that you enjoy.

Simple, Cute and Shy

This type of girl usually has the following characteristics

- Has very little exposure to the outside world. Her world usually revolves around home, family and a small circle of friends.
- In case she is working, then it is usually at a 9 to 5 low/moderate income and zero stress job.
- Is not very ambitious or career-oriented.
- Has over protective and usually very strict parents.
- Looks cute and has a happy go lucky nature.

- ✦ Is shy and her social skills are not well developed.
- ✦ Usually lives in a small city and rides a moped or scooter.

In mid-2014, I got in touch with a girl based in Pune. She used to work part time as a lecturer and was also studying for her master's degree. She seemed very shy, sweet and had a cute childlike innocence to her.

Once while talking to her on the phone, she mentioned to me that her birthday was approaching in a few months time. I casually asked her what she would like as a gift for her birthday. I was expecting that she might ask for something expensive like jewelry or shoes. Instead she asked me for a box of crayons and a sketching book as she was very artistic. I was simply stunned by this simple request of hers and it made my heart melt. This was one of those moments in life which really make you pause and wonder that we as adults are so busy chasing money, status and success that we often forget the simple joys of life.

After a few weeks, her mom insisted that they match our horoscopes (I still don't understand why people in India are so obsessed with horoscope matching) before proceeding further. Since our horoscopes did not match her mother told her to stop talking to me. Knowing this girl well by now, I knew that she would not dare to disobey her mother. I wished her good luck and that was the last I heard from her.

Key tip: Girls should learn to be more assertive, develop social skills and make their decisions themselves.

Factors Which Influence The Marriage Decision

There are many factors that influence the marriage decision making process in India. Marriage decision making process often tends to be quite complex. In my opinion many (if not all) of these factors tend to be beyond the control of any single individual. The following chapters discuss some of the factors I personally experienced.

The Caste System and Language

Even today the caste system retains a vice-like grip on the Indian marriage system. I personally feel that there should be no caste system. While I belong to the Brahmin caste, I would have no problems marrying a girl from any caste whatsoever, if I felt she was good enough for me. It's not in the hands of a person, what sort of caste they will be born into.

If you think I would have it easy because I supposedly belong to a high caste, then you are completely wrong. On top of the caste system, there is something called as a sub-caste. A friend of my parents had a daughter who was a couple of years younger to me. My parents were insistent that they approach them since they knew her family for over 20 years. After some convincing, I agreed to email my photos and bio-data to the girl.

We were later informed that the girl's mother did not want to proceed further, as she only wanted a groom who was not only Brahmin but also belonged to the same Brahmin sub caste as them. This really had to be the height of stupidity for turning down an otherwise perfectly good marriage proposal.

In addition to the caste system, language or mother tongue plays a significant role too. In India there are over a dozen major languages and even more number of dialects. Practically each state has its own language. In USA, English is by far the most commonly used language and all the business occurs mostly in English (Spanish is used increasingly in order to cater to the growing Hispanic population). The only difference is that depending on the region you are living in, the accents do vary.

Human beings inherently prefer people who can speak a common language as it makes it easier to communicate. I know only know Marathi, Hindi, English and Gujarati. So as a personal choice I would prefer a spouse who has at least one language in common. Her mother tongue may be different from the above mentioned languages, but I would be fine with that.

Key point: Do not accept or reject a person solely based on his or her caste.

Horoscope/Kundali Matching

Horoscope matching is one of those things which can almost singlehandedly make or break the marriage decision process. I personally do not believe much in it, but I can't tell you how many people I know (including many in my own family), believe it to the point of fanaticism. Since I am a manglik, I am as toxic as nuclear radioactive waste for any non manglik girl. Merely talking with me might be enough to kill her (just joking). Since mangliks are in a minority, life for us isn't easy while looking for a spouse.

In mid-2014, I had expressed interest in a Mumbai based girl, which was promptly accepted. She was tall, good looking and had a great smile. She had worked as a counselor at a leading hospital in Mumbai for a couple of years before quitting to start her own fashion design venture. She had travelled abroad and seemed to have a great personality. By all counts she looked to be the perfect kind of girl for me.

We started chatting online after she accepted my interest on the matrimonial site. Barely had we exchanged some initial information, when she asked for my date of birth, place of birth and time of birth. I understood that this information was being asked for the purposes of horoscope matching. I was told she and her family strongly believed in horoscope matching, and they had their own *panditji* who would be visiting their house next week. He, in his infinite wisdom would alone decide our fates. Until then there was going to be no further talking, no phone calls or what's app.

I nervously waited for a week to hear the good news from her. I was secretly hoping that our horoscopes would match perfectly so that we live together happily ever after. A week went by and then she texted me *Panditji's* decision. *Panditji* had come to the conclusion that since I was manglik and she was not, our marriage was not possible. Should we defy him and marry, the entire universe would fall apart.

After a few messages back and forth she reluctantly agreed to talk with me on the phone. I tried to make her realize that we should still meet up and talk face to face to see if there is compatibility between us but despite my best attempts this girl would not budge. She was absolutely adamant that we would not talk anymore.

Back in USA, I was able to convince some of the toughest Fortune 500 clients using my power of persuasion and negotiation. I can only hope that she can find a guy whose horoscope would match perfectly with hers and she can receive *panditji's* approval.

Key tip: Believing only in horoscope with complete disregard for all the other factors is a recipe for disaster.

Financial Expectations

Money or the lack of it plays a very important role in practically every relationship.

Almost every girl expects that the guy should be earning very well. Previous sections of this book have already elaborated on my experiences when dealing with girls and their families. Based on my observations, the minimum package a guy must have in Tier 1 city in India is 15 lakhs per annum.

Expectations are even higher if the guy is working abroad. In 2013 while I was still living in USA, I happened to chat with a girl based in Surat. After we had chatted a couple of times, she asked me how much my income was. It was around $70,000 per annum including base salary, bonuses and other benefits. I was living in a city in Upstate New York and this income was quite good (not excellent) by American standards based on the local cost of living. She mentioned that some of the other marriage proposals she had received had guys making about $90,000 to $100,000 per year in New York City. I understood that she was hinting that I did not make enough money as compared to them. I was pretty annoyed at this and wished her good luck in her search. In her greed to find a guy who could make as much money as possible, she (and possibly her parents) was completely ignoring the cost of living factor.

For those of you who are unfamiliar with how things work in USA, here is a little explanation. In USA, cost of living varies significantly based on the geographical location. For the city I was living in, I paid about $800 per month in rent for a very nice 1 bedroom & bathroom apartment. The area of the apartment was over 600 square feet which is very good for a single person or even a married couple. In NYC similar apartment would cost you at least $2,000 in rent. In case you have a car, parking charges add another $200 to $500 a month. Where I lived, the parking was free. So $70,000 in Upstate New York would be equivalent to nearly $120,000 to 150,000 in NYC.

As you can see I was making more money in a year *relatively speaking.* You can check this online using cost of living calculator and you will see the logic of my argument. The trouble is many people (especially greedy ones) simply do not understand logic no matter how hard you try to explain it to them.

The issue of money in relationships is a worldwide problem regardless of nationality or religion. One of my American friends who was dating a Chinese girl shared his experience with me.

"She was just very cold emotionally, and was completely set on ultra-conservative Chinese traditions that a relationship first and foremost is when the husband supports her and her immediate family financially, and that maybe she would fall in love with the guy as long as she and her family are completely financially secure (she asked what my credit score was on the 3rd date, right, hahaha!). It's always great to hear that a good friend agrees with my point of view that this last girl's views were completely ridiculous and unreasonable. Sorry to hear that you've been running into similar issues with girls and money too. Frankly, I think that you're a better man than a lot of people over in India just based on the fact that you have experienced what it is really like in America, and have a wiser more realistic world view and perspective as a result.

It seems there are that a lot of good looking girls who know they're hot, and use their looks to take advantage of guys. I have to admit though, I am grateful that you and I are not tied down in a relationship with a girl who likes me as long as I make money. I know quite a few people with this problem who are miserable."

Up until 1991, India was a mostly socialist economy with government directly or indirectly controlling most of the economy with some private sector involvement. Since the last couple of decades, as India gets more and more privatized, lifelong job security is increasingly going to be a thing of the past. It does not matter which field you are working in or what are your educational qualifications; you can be laid off due to factors beyond your control. For example in July 2014, Microsoft Corporation alone announced a layoff of 18,000 employees [2]. Many Indian IT companies also layoff thousands of employees each year.

Imagine that you are a man aged 30. You had graduated from a good engineering college and were hired by a leading IT company through campus recruitment when you were 22. For the next 7 or 8 years your career moved ahead smoothly and you started to specialized in certain software or coding languages, because your employer told you to do so. Your package nearly touches 20 lakhs per annum. Somewhere along the way, you found a match and the girl looking at your good steady job at a "big MNC" says yes. You get married and after a year or so have a kid. Things start to change on the job front as your employer's customer no longer needs or uses the software domain knowledge you have. After a few months on the bench you are fired by the HR department. Your home loan, car EMI and maybe even your marriage are in trouble.

The above scenario has been repeating itself for the past few years and will increasingly get common in the future. If you are about to marry someone because he or she has this well paid job at XYZ corporation, then you need to be aware that there are no guarantees that the job will always be there forever.

Key tip: While making a marriage decision, always remember a good job today is no guarantee of perpetual financial security.

Role Of Matrimonial Websites

For most people finding a good spouse was never easy or straightforward. Other than the usual channels of parents, relatives, extended family, *panditji* and possibly through college or University it was difficult to find good prospects. Newspaper matrimonial ads were also used to search for potential spouses. The trouble with the newspaper ads is that they are too short and have no photographs. It is said that a picture is worth a thousand words.

Some communities also publish various booklets containing details about prospective brides and grooms for interested parties to contact each other. One of my overenthusiastic uncles (doesn't every family have someone like this?) once scanned the entire booklet and emailed it to me even though I had not asked for it. The funny thing was that it was written in Gujarati which I cannot read or write despite it being my mother tongue.

In the last decade or so, online matrimonial sites have increased significantly. Anyone can create a nice profile in a few minutes and upload a few good photographs of themselves. This opens up huge new possibilities for meeting people whom you would have not otherwise met. Just because there are so many people using these sites, it does not automatically guarantee that you will find a good match there. Previous pages of this book have already elaborated on my experiences using such sites.

Here are some of the pros and cons of such websites based on my experience.

Pros

- A very large and growing database of potential spouses (new members join every single day).
- Can save a lot of time and effort as most of the information is available at your fingertips.
- Given the intense competition between various websites, the membership fees are reasonable. Once you are a member significant discounts are usually offered for renewal of memberships.
- You can narrow down the search criteria using a wide number of parameters such as age, height, geographic location, language etc.

Cons

- While these websites often show a few success stories, they do not publish detailed statistics such as total number of members, success rate by city or region etc.

- These websites are only as good as the quality of people (members) and the way they use the website.
- Even though the database is large, many profiles are inactive. I personally came across hundreds of profiles that had been inactive for over 2 or 3 months. Website administrators should delete such profiles.
- It is very easy to make any profile sound very impressive easily and make you look someone who you aren't really.

Below are some simple suggestions for everyone using these websites.

- Create a good profile with enough basic information about yourself such as your educational and work background, family details and your partner expectations. Do not blabber too much or make it too lengthy to read.
- Please post at least 4 or 5 good quality photographs of yourself. Do not edit or Photoshop your photos. It will save your and everyone else's time. I *do not* accept any interests if they do not have photos attached to their profile.
- You are a grown up adult so manage your profile on your own. Asking parents, relatives or siblings to manage your profile is not a good idea.

- If you do accept someone's interest then be prompt in responding by email or phone.
- Get to know the person well before agreeing to meet him/her in person.

Key tip: Online matrimonial sites offer a good way to meet potential spouses; you should create a good profile and must be able to manage it properly.

Role Of Marriage Agents Or Matchmakers

As I celebrated my 29th birthday without a spouse by my side, by parents increasingly began to fret. As most people will know, family pressures in India can be quite intense. One of my dad's friends had told him about this reputed "marriage agent/ matchmaker". He claimed to have a huge database of well qualified guys and girls with many of them being professional from well to do business families. After constant nagging from my parents, I sent him my bio-data and a few photographs. I was asked to pay an initial fee of INR 11,000 which I paid. This wasn't a big amount for me considering all the claims he was making.

He sent me the bio-data of a few girls along with their photographs. I was further told that I could not directly contact any of these girls and their contact details were absent from their bio-data. I informed him about the girls I liked and he set up a date with one of the girls after a few days. Under normal situations I would have tried to get a better idea regarding the person I was meeting before the actual meeting.

The date was set at a coffee shop on a Friday evening. I was just about to leave my home for the date; I received a call from an unknown number. I answered the call and realized that it was from my date. She was having tooth problems and was unable to meet me. When your date calls you 30 minutes before the meeting with a toothache, it definitely raises your suspicions. Nevertheless I decided to give her the benefit of doubt and rescheduled the meeting for Saturday evening.

The date was a disaster. First, the girl showed up 30 minutes late. Upon seeing her I was surprised (not in a good way) as she looked very different from her photos. She was shorter and overweight compared to the photos that were sent to me. I had a feeling that either her photos were several years old or were probably photo shopped. Her body language suggested that she had been pressurized to meet me. I further observed that her lower front teeth were indeed in a very bad shape along with several other teeth. Barely 20 minutes after arrival, she received a phone call and left in a hurry, without even shaking my hand or saying goodbye. Her lack of manners did not impress me.

Just a couple of days later I received a call from this agent asking for another hefty payment as he had set up the previous meeting. He was also promising to set up more meetings with other girls once I had paid this amount. My gut instinct was telling me that this agent was no good, and I firmly told him that I was not interested in using his services anymore.

Matchmaking is a fairly lucrative profession and every Tom, Dick and Harry wants to give it a shot. The investment required is practically zero. This can result in a high possibility for a scam wherein multiple families could be taken for a ride by asking them to pay hefty amounts of money for a very questionable service. These agents might themselves create dozens or even hundreds of fake profiles in order to make things look far better than they actually are.

There could be some agents who are genuinely successful in getting people to meet. If you choose to use the services of such agents, then ask them to provide you with testimonials from recent success stories. If possible do ask for the phone numbers of couples who have actually married after being put in touch by the agent to verify their claims. While there is probably no legal restriction on the amount of fees these agents can charge, if you feel their fees are high or unreasonable, then *do not pay.*

Key tip: Try to avoid using the services of marriage agents. Verify beforehand if you decide to use their services.

Factors To Consider In A Potential Spouse

This part of the book deals with factors that one should consider before making marriage decisions. Some of them are personal and may or may not be applicable to you. Since this book is written for a wide audience you can choose to ignore any of the factors if they do not apply to you.

It has been previously discussed in this book that there are factors in life over which an individual does not have any control. However the factors being discussed below are important as most of them are due to choices you have personally made. For example, if you are a smoker then it is because you choose to smoke. Nobody has forced you to smoke.

The good news with these factors is that you can still make wise choices and reduce or eliminate most of these lifestyle factors. This section presents a lot of medical information which has been taken from highly reputed American and British medical institutions in order to maintain the integrity of this book and convince the reader of this book to take such information seriously.

Obesity and Overweight

Obesity levels in India have reached alarming proportions. It is estimated that nearly 5% of the population of India is morbidly obese [3]. If the current population of India is about 1.2 billion that translates to nearly 6 crore people! To put it differently, that's more people than the entire population of National Capital Region (NCR) of India.

The most common way to measure if any adult is overweight or obese is through body mass index (BMI). It is calculated by taking a person's weight in kilograms (kg) divided by his or her height in meters squared. The following chart shows if a person is underweight, normal weight, overweight or obese. [4]

Underweight	=	<18.5
Normal weight	=	18.5–24.9
Overweight	=	25–29.9
Obesity	=	BMI of 30 or greater

While living in USA, I had observed many people make a New Year's resolution to lose weight. During Thanksgiving and Christmas holidays people there eat a lot and then they realize that they must get back in shape. Gyms also offer attractive packages in order to entice new members. Come January, and I used to see packed gyms. As March approaches the numbers begin to decline and by May gyms used to be more or less empty.

Even in my neighborhood gym in Mumbai, I see many people trying hard to lose weight without any diet changes. If you indeed want to lose weight and maintain fitness, you need a proper combination of exercise, diet and personal habits. In addition to this, you will also need patience, determination and commitment towards your fitness goals. In today's world people just expect everything instantly.

In the worst case scenario, extremely obese people often have to resort to measures such as Bariatric surgery when everything else has failed. Any sort of surgical procedure comes with its own set of complications. Wouldn't it be much better and easier for people to keep their BMI within normal range?

According to National Heart, Lung and Blood Institute (USA), following are some of the health hazards of being overweight or obese [4]

Coronary Heart Disease

As your body mass index rises, so does your risk for coronary heart disease (CHD). CHD is a condition in which a waxy substance called plaque builds up inside the coronary arteries. These arteries supply oxygen-rich blood to your heart.

Plaque can narrow or block the coronary arteries and reduce blood flow to the heart muscles. This can cause angina or a heart attack. (Angina is chest pain or discomfort.)

Obesity can also lead to heart failure. This is a serious condition in which your heart can't pump enough blood to meet your body's needs.

High Blood Pressure

Blood pressure is the force of blood pushing against the walls of the arteries as the heart pumps blood. If this pressure rises and stays high over time, it can damage the body in many ways.

Your chances of having high blood pressure are greater if you›re overweight or obese.

Stroke

Being overweight or obese can lead to a buildup of plaque in your arteries. Eventually, an area of plaque can rupture, causing a blood clot to form.

If the clot is close to your brain, it can block the flow of blood and oxygen to your brain and cause a stroke. The risk of having a stroke rises as BMI increases.

Type 2 Diabetes

Diabetes is a disease in which the body's blood glucose, or blood sugar, level is too high. Normally, the body breaks down food into glucose and then carries it to cells throughout the body. The cells use a hormone called insulin to turn the glucose into energy.

In type 2 diabetes, the body's cells don't use insulin properly. At first, the body reacts by making more insulin. Over time, however, the body can't make enough insulin to control its blood sugar level.

Diabetes is a leading cause of early death, CHD, stroke, kidney disease, and blindness. Most people who have type 2 diabetes are overweight.

Abnormal Blood Fats

If you're overweight or obese, you're at increased risk of having abnormal levels of blood fats. These include high levels of triglycerides and LDL ("bad") cholesterol and low levels of HDL ("good") cholesterol.

Abnormal levels of these blood fats are a risk factor for CHD.

Cancer

Being overweight or obese raises your risk for colon, breast, endometrial, and gallbladder cancers.

Osteoarthritis

Osteoarthritis is a common joint problem of the knees, hips and lower back. The condition occurs if the tissue that protects the joints wears away. Extra weight can put more pressure and wear on joints, causing pain.

Reproductive problems

Obesity can cause menstrual issues and infertility in women.

If a person is overweight or obese while he/she is young, in the 20s, then his weight will only increase as he gets older. If you do marry such a person and have kids in future, chances of these children having health issues are automatically increased. I feel that you owe a gift of good health to your future children. As this book has previously discussed, childhood obesity is rising in many countries around the world.

Key tip: Do not agree to marry overweight or obese persons until they make a firm commitment to reduce their weight. Make sure they back their commitment with action.

Medical History

It is strongly recommended that both of you should be in good physical, mental and emotional health before getting married. The guy and the girl should get a complete health checkup before getting married (including checking for sexually transmitted diseases). *While this might sound harsh to some people, it's better to be safe than sorry.*

According to National Institutes of Health, U.S. National Library of Medicine, some of the most common tests for adults in their 20s and 30s are [6]

- Blood pressure screening
- Cholesterol screening
- Diabetes screening
- Dental exam (you want a bright smile in the wedding photos!)
- Eye exam(if you have vision problems)
- Immunizations
- Physical exam
- Infectious disease screening
- Pelvic exam and pap smear for women

Key tip: The girl and the guy should undergo complete medical checkup before marriage.

Smoking

An old but true statement about cigarettes is "A pinch of tobacco rolled in paper with fire at one end and a fool at the other." India has about 11 crore smokers (110 million). [7] These days smoking cigarettes has become a fashion statement among many young urban educated people. Take a walk outside any big office building/business park during lunch break, and you will see dozens and maybe even hundreds of well-dressed and highly educated young men and women smoking. Since their education did not teach them the risks of smoking, I have dedicated the next couple of pages to point out the health risks of smoking.

According to National Health Service (United Kingdom), smoking increases your risk of developing more than 50 serious health conditions. Some may be fatal and others can cause irreversible long-term damage to your health. [8]

You can become ill:

- if you smoke yourself
- through other people's smoke (passive smoking, or secondhand smoke)

Health risks

Smoking causes about 90% of lung cancers. It also causes cancer in many other parts of the body, including the:

- mouth
- lips
- throat
- voice box (larynx)
- oesophagus (the tube between your mouth and stomach)
- bladder
- kidney
- liver
- stomach
- pancreas

Smoking damages your heart and your blood circulation, increasing your risk of developing conditions such as:

- coronary heart disease
- heart attack
- stroke
- peripheral vascular disease (damaged blood vessels)
- cerebrovascular disease (damaged arteries that supply blood to your brain)

Smoking also damages your lungs, leading to conditions such as:

- chronic bronchitis (infection of the main airways in the lungs)

- emphysema (damage to the small airways in the lungs)
- pneumonia (inflammation in the lungs)

Secondhand smoke

Secondhand smoke comes from the tip of a lit cigarette and the smoke that the smoker breathes out.

People who breathe in secondhand smoke are at risk of getting the same health conditions as smokers, particularly lung cancer and heart disease. For example, breathing in secondhand smoke increases a non-smoker's risk of developing lung cancer or heart disease by about 25%.

Smoking during pregnancy

If you smoke when you're pregnant, you put your unborn baby's health at risk, as well as your own. Smoking during pregnancy increases the risk of complications such as:

- miscarriage
- premature (early) birth
- a low birth weight baby
- stillbirth

While it isn't impossible, addiction to smoking can be hard to break. If you indeed want to marry a smoker despite all the health risks, I can only suggest that you make him/her undergo a de-addiction program.

Chewing tobacco or Gutka is equally dangerous for health and must be avoided. Gutka is a combination of areca nut, slaked lime, paraffin and katechu along with tobacco. This mixture is a combination of 4,000 chemicals of which at least 40 are carcinogenic compounds.[9]

Key tip: Given all the health risks of smoking, this is a no brainer. Do not marry a smoker.

Excessive Drinking

First of all I am not against drinking per se. A fine wine can complement a nice meal at a restaurant. But many people are unable to draw a line between drinking occasionally and drinking too much.

According to National Institute on Alcohol Abuse and Alcoholism, drinking too much – on a single occasion or over time – can take a serious toll on your health [10]. Here's how alcohol can affect your body:

Brain:

Alcohol interferes with the brain's communication pathways, and can affect the way the brain looks and works. These disruptions can change mood and behavior, and make it harder to think clearly and move with coordination.

Heart:

Drinking a lot over a long time or too much on a single occasion can damage the heart, causing problems including:

- Cardiomyopathy – Stretching and drooping of heart muscle
- Arrhythmia – Irregular heart beat
- Stroke
- High blood pressure

Liver:

Heavy drinking takes a toll on the liver, and can lead to a variety of problems and liver inflammations including:

- Steatosis, or fatty liver
- Alcoholic hepatitis
- Fibrosis
- Cirrhosis

Pancreas:

Alcohol causes the pancreas to produce toxic substances that can eventually lead to pancreatitis, a dangerous inflammation and swelling of the blood vessels in the pancreas that prevents proper digestion.

Cancer:

Drinking too much alcohol can increase your risk of developing certain cancers, including cancers of the:

- Mouth
- Esophagus
- Throat
- Liver
- Breast

Immune system:

Drinking too much can weaken your immune system, making your body a much easier target for disease. Chronic drinkers are more liable to contract diseases like pneumonia and tuberculosis than people who do not drink too much. Drinking a lot on a single occasion slows your body's ability to ward off infections – even up to 24 hours after getting drunk.

Excessive drinking and driving a motor vehicle thereafter, is serious problem everywhere around the world. It can injure or kill not only you but also other vehicle users and pedestrians. According to Department of Transportation (USA), National Highway Traffic Safety Administration (NHTSA) in 2013; 10,076 people were killed in alcohol-impaired driving crashes in the United States. [11]

If you are caught drinking and driving then your driving license can be suspended and you can be sent to jail. Following is the data collected from Mumbai Traffic Police website regarding drunk driving in Mumbai. [12]

Achievements

Since 1st January 2015 to 20th May 2015

Total Cases registered	6,067
Imprisonment for Drunk Driving	2,175
MDL/Licenses suspended by Hon.Court	1,186
Fine Collected in Rupees	1,16,38,150

Source:http://trafficpolicemumbai.maharashtra.gov.in/cloud/ocms.aspx?id=1001201#

Key tip: Make sure your future spouse does not drink alcohol in excess. Teetotalers are an even better option.

Drug Use

In the past few years, recreational drug use has increased among a certain section of the society. Media does report from time to time how police raided a popular nightclub or a rave party and arrested several people who were caught using or in possession of banned drugs. Unlike smoking or drinking, drug use is illegal and you can get into serious trouble with the law.

In USA, some employers do ask for drug testing for existing as well as potential employees if they are being considered for a particular position. If a person tests positive for drugs then they can be fired from their job. Employers can offer a job contingent on you passing the drug test. If you fail, then the job offer is rescinded. The rules are strict and there are no exceptions. One of my batch mates in USA, who is an MBA, was hired to work for a defense contractor, and even he had to undergo drug testing despite his excellent background and qualifications.

According to National Institute on Drug Abuse, Drug addiction is a brain disease.[13] Although initial drug use might be voluntary, abuse of drugs has been shown to alter gene expression and brain circuitry, which in turn affect human behavior. Once addiction develops, these brain changes interfere with an individual's ability to make voluntary decisions, leading to compulsive drug craving, seeking and use.

The impact of addiction can be far reaching. Cardiovascular disease, stroke, cancer, HIV/AIDS, hepatitis, and lung disease can all be caused by drug abuse. Some of these effects occur when drugs are used at high doses or after prolonged use; however, some may occur after just one use.

Key tip: Anyone who uses drugs is a strict NO!

Age & Height

A person's age and height are unalterable factors. They might not sound very important but actually play a fairly important role in selecting a spouse. These cannot be changed later no matter how much you try.

Most women prefer that their husbands should be taller than them and almost every guy wants his wife to be shorter in height than him. Couples with taller woman and shorter guy are very rare. I personally would not prefer a girl who is taller than me.

Traditionally it has been preferred that the woman be a few years younger than her husband. The reason for this is that girls usually mature faster than boys. There are marriages wherein the partners have a significant age difference (a decade of more) between them, but the marriage is still successful. Maturity and personal preferences are important with regard to age and height of your future spouse.

It is also said that age is just a number. There are many people who are young but they do not take care of themselves in any way and there are people who are older but they maintain good health. Being young at heart is important as you should be able to laugh and be like a kid sometimes. In general, most adults smile very little, let alone laugh.

In late 2009 my American roommate's parents visited our apartment. His dad was in his mid-60s and his mom was in her early 60s. Both of them looked much younger than their age. My point here is that you can look and feel younger at any age if you have a good attitude and maintain a healthy lifestyle.

Key tip: Be clear on what your expectations are with regard to age and height of your future spouse.

Eating Habits

A large percentage of population in India is still strictly vegetarian. In Mumbai many housing societies do not even permit non vegetarians to buy flats. Certain communities in India do not even eat vegetables such as onions and garlic. Whether you are vegetarian or non-vegetarian, you should eat a nutritious and well balanced diet.

In USA large number of people have turned vegetarian or even vegan in the last decade or so. People who follow a vegan diet do not eat any animal products including milk, cheese or yogurt. Plant based substitutes such as soy milk, almond milk and coconut milk are used in place of animal products.

While it might sound trivial, many vegetarians I know of cannot even stand the sight of eggs, let alone any type of meat. So whether you are vegetarian or non-vegetarian can influence your decision regarding selecting a spouse.

One of the biggest problems of an all vegetarian diet is that the daily protein intake is usually low. Protein is the building block of the body. If you are a hardcore vegetarian, then taking protein supplements such as whey or casein (which are milk based) can help you reach your recommended dietary allowance for protein.

According to Centers for Disease Prevention and Control (USA) it's recommended that 10–35% of your daily calories come from protein. Below are the Recommended Dietary Allowances (RDA) for different age groups. [14]

Recommended Dietary Allowance for Protein	
	Grams of protein needed each day
Children ages 1 – 3	13
Children ages 4 – 8	19
Children ages 9 – 13	34
Girls ages 14 – 18	46
Boys ages 14 – 18	52
Women ages 19 – 70+	46
Men ages 19 – 70+	56

Here are examples of amounts of protein in food:

- 1 cup of milk has 8 grams of protein
- A 3-ounce piece of meat has about 21 grams of protein
- 1 cup of dry beans has about 16 grams of protein
- An 8-ounce container of yogurt has about 11 grams of protein

Added together, just these four sources would meet the protein needs of an adult male (56 grams). This doesn't count all the other foods that add smaller amounts of protein to his diet.

Key tip: You should be comfortable with your spouse's dietary habits.

Past Relationships

Sex before marriage is considered to be taboo in India. There is still a large percentage of population especially in smaller cities and rural areas which is quite conservative. However in almost every big city in India couples openly date each other. There are several spots in Mumbai alone, especially near the sea coast, where one can find couples holding hands and kissing in full public view every day. While it is common in western countries, a couple living together before marriage is still not acceptable to a large section of Indian society.

Many people feel it's a good idea to lie about your past. Any relationship based on lies never lasts. You must be mentally, emotionally and physically ready for marriage. You want to start marriage which is supposedly going to be a lifelong relationship on a positive note. If you and your potential spouse do not wish to discuss each other's pasts, then it's your choice. If you do, then you might want to ask the following questions. Please remember to keep such discussions strictly confidential between you and your potential spouse.

- How many relationships was the person in?
- How long were those relationships?
- Was sex involved?
- Did it result in unintended pregnancy or abortion?
- What was the reason for break up or it not working out?
- Is the person completely over the ex-girlfriend/ boyfriend?

Human relationships are complex. Bad relationships can often hurt a person mentally and emotionally. If a person has jumped from relationship to relationship, it shows an unstable and unreliable nature. This sort of behavior combined with habits such as smoking or drinking clearly raises a red flag.

You are probably better off by not being with such a person.

Let's consider two hypothetical scenarios

Nisha is in a relationship with her boyfriend Anil. Her parents find a well settled guy from a wealthy family (let's call him Mohan) for her. She decides to dump Anil who is of modest means for Mohan. Enraged at her betrayal Anil stabs Nisha to death in a fit of rage. Her parents are left grieving over her death and Anil is arrested.

Ramesh is in a relationship with his girlfriend Sunita but they are unable to get married because of differences in their caste. His parents insist on finding a girl from within their community. He somehow agrees to marry a girl (let's call her Priyanka) of his parents' choice. Even after his marriage to Priyanka, he completely ignores her and continues his affair with Sunita. After many frustrating months, Priyanka goes back to her parents' house and files for divorce. Priyanka suffers so much anguish for no fault of her own.

Similar cases are being reported at an alarming rate in the media. Several popular reality shows on Indian television shows are full of criminal cases happening because of love triangles and spurned lovers. Many marriages in India are still arranged under family pressure (family pressure can be quite intense in India), and the girl or guy is still in love with someone else.

Such things are avoidable with a little understanding from all sides. Parents can reason and make their child understand why they feel that a particular person is not a good choice to be a spouse for him/her, instead of using pressure or scare tactics. Parents should make their children aware when they are teenagers, about good and bad choices.

If you are a grown up adult in true love with someone, and that person also loves you back (true love is very different compared to just being infatuated with someone), then laws in India do give you a legal right to go ahead and marry. If you do go against your family, then it is possible that they may never support you in future. Think about the consequences of your actions and then act accordingly.

Key tip: Do not hide anything about your past from your future spouse. You must be mentally, emotionally and physically ready for marriage.

Sexual Orientation

As a grown up adult one should be clear about one's sexual orientation. You should be aware whether you are a homosexual or a heterosexual person. If you have doubts or need any medical advice then you should seek help from a counsellor or a doctor. There are several NGOs who might be able to help you.

As of June 2015, Homosexuality is a criminal offence in India under section 377. *My only advice would be that do not agree to a heterosexual marriage if you are a homosexual.*

Key tip: If you are a homosexual then please do not ruin someone else's life by entering into a heterosexual marriage.

Educational Attainment

Educational attainment refers to the highest level of education (degree) that an individual has completed. It can also have a qualitative aspect to it. For example, a degree obtained from Ivy League universities is usually considered to be prestigious in USA. Similarly a degree from Indian Institutes of Technology (IIT) and Indian Institutes of Management (IIM) are held in high standing by many people and employers.

Intellectual level and educational attainment is usually co-related. Higher education exposes you to new knowledge, new ways of thinking and doing things. If a girl is well educated then she will have a hard time being with a guy who does not match or exceed her education level. Similar situation exists for guys too.

Education, while important, is not the only thing. A person maybe brilliant academically and successful professionally, but should also be humble and have a personality such that other people would be able to relate to him or her. It took even me a while to learn this.

As a part of my job, I often had to undertake site visits to large commercial and industrial customers. This involved meeting senior managers in plush offices in NYC to meeting mechanics and workers on the factory floor in heavy industry. I had to win over and convince these people in order to get the work done in a professional way. My degree from a top ranked US university was more or less useless in such situations. People should see you as a humble person who is trying to do his job while helping them along the way.

Instead of being only academically smart, a person should also be street smart and show willingness to learn new things. One of my uncles is a PhD but he doesn't have even an iota of common sense in him, and it's difficult to deal with him even during normal situations. Fortunately for him (and all other family members) my aunt (she is a PhD too) is a gem of a person and she is able to handle him properly.

Key tip: Educational attainment is a good (though not the only) thing to have in a future spouse.

Looks, Grooming and Personal Hygiene

People in India are obsessed with white/fair skin. A massive fairness cream industry exists in order to cater to the need of the people to look white. Fairness cream industry in India generates thousands of crores of rupees in revenue every year (equivalent to hundreds of millions of dollars). Earlier fairness creams were only targeted towards women, but these days some companies even have products for men to look *gora* (white). It is almost impossible to permanently change the complexion you were born with just by applying some fairness cream.

I feel that fair skin alone is not a measure of beauty. Since I was living in USA for many years, I had to interact with Americans on a daily basis. Many of these people were very fair in complexion but not otherwise attractive. Things such as overweight/obesity, lack of education and smoking certainly made them less likeable. It is said that a healthy mind lives in a healthy body. If you are not fit and reasonably active, then your complexion will not matter much. A girl who is not fair but is in shape, is far more attractive than a girl with fair complexion but out of shape.

Beauty is not just skin deep, but things such as a person's personality, intelligence, character and attitude also matter a lot. In USA, dumb blonde jokes are very common. Dumb blonde jokes refer to a physically attractive woman (who has blonde hair) but who is completely clueless about the world around her and often behaves in a comical/stupid way.

My friend's sister-in-law had shared a valuable piece of advice a few years ago which I still remember. She had said looks don't matter much after a few months into marriage. You see a person in every way once you are married from being sleepy in the morning to being tired after a long day at work. Initial beauty fades and a person's good qualities start to matter a lot more. She did say you want someone who maintains good health and looks presentable outside the house.

While people in India are more or less contented with using fairness creams to look white, a far larger medical industrial complex exists in many other countries. People often go to great lengths to make themselves look more beautiful. In many countries, plastic surgery is a big industry and surgeries such as liposuction, nose job, lip job, breast implants etc. are quite common. Some Bollywood celebrities have gone under the knife often with not so desirable results. If you want to consider plastic surgery then please understand the risks and consult with your doctor.

Some of dangers associated with plastic surgery came out when a French company called Poly Implant Prothèse (PIP) which made silicone gel breast implants was preemptively liquidated in 2010 following the revelation that they had been illegally manufacturing and selling breast implants made from cheaper industrial-grade silicone since 2001 (instead of the mandated medical-grade silicone they had previously used). The hundreds of thousands of unapproved implants sold globally by PIP from 2001 to 2010 were found to have a 500% higher risk of rupturing than approved models, as well as being implicated in several deaths due to systemic toxicity and several cases of induced breast cancer. The scandal, which produced fears of a massive health disaster, prompted a full recall of the company's implants by the French health ministry in 2010. [15]

Maintaining good personal hygiene is essential at a personal and professional level. I still come across people who do not even follow simple day to day rules on personal hygiene. The lack of personal hygiene can cause many illnesses to you as well as your co-workers and family members. Here are some of the rules one must follow daily in order to maintain personal hygiene.

- A daily shower is a must whether you like it or not.
- Washing hands with soap before and after eating food.
- Washing hands with soap after using the toilet.
- Keeping your finger and toe nails trimmed and in good shape.
- Cleaning your ears regularly to remove ear wax.
- Brush & floss every day. If you have bad breath then use a mouth fresher or mouth wash. See your dentist to maintain good oral health.
- Take care of your hair and wash it once or twice a week. Use hair oil if you wish to.
- Undesirable hair anywhere on your body should be trimmed or shaved.
- Use a good deodorant, body spray or perfume to keep body odor under control. Do not apply it in excess; the smell should not be so strong as to bother other people around you.
- Do not share your towel with anyone and wash your towel with detergent regularly.
- Try to sleep well every night.

Grooming is not absolutely necessary but a well-groomed person is always more attractive than a shabby person. Grooming also conveys a person's taste and sophistication. Here are some grooming tips which should make you feel good about yourself.

- Invest in good fashionable clothes. A large wardrobe is not necessary. A few good clothes should be enough.
- Clothes should not look cheap, ill-fitting or awkward.
- Develop a general idea regarding fashion trends.
- Invest in good fragrances (colognes, after shave lotions and body sprays).
- Use good quality skin care products (not fairness creams!) to keep your skin smooth and to prevent dryness and itchiness of the skin.
- Good comfortable shoes are essential. Have different pairs of shoes for different uses such as running shoes, casual shoes, formal shoes and sandals/slippers.
- For women a good handbag is a must. Some classy jewelry can add a nice touch to your overall appearance. Avoid excessive or gaudy jewelry.
- Avoid using excessive make up.

- Since Indian weather very hot and sunny, a good pair of sunglasses can make you look stylish and protect your eyes from ultra violet (UV) rays whenever you are outside. Please do not wear them indoors!

Key tip: Looks are important but one should not be obsessed about them. Maintaining good personal hygiene is very important. Bonus points for well-groomed persons.

Common Interests

Spending enough time together is very important for any relationship. There is a saying "out of sight, out of mind" which means that you soon forget people or things that are no longer visible or present. Sharing some common interests/activities is helpful for long term success in a marriage. It is also exciting and breaks the day to day monotony. The activities should be fun, stress busting and not be too physically demanding.

- Gym
- Yoga
- Outdoors – hiking, trekking, picnics, cycling/ biking
- Wine tasting

- Travelling around the world and seeing new places
- Trying out new restaurants and cuisines
- Movies
- Dancing
- Music (if you can play any musical instrument well, then it's a good thing)
- Hobbies such as painting, crafts, collecting coins or stamps
- Pets (if you like animals)

There are very adventurous activities such as sky diving, bungee jumping, white water rafting etc. which can be very demanding physically and can be scary for many people. You should avoid such activities if you do not feel comfortable doing them.

Key tip: Doing together the activities that you both enjoy is a good way to bond and be close to one another.

Behavior

People's behavior speaks volumes about the way they were raised by their parents. Behaviour can give a lot of insight into the kind of person an individual is, and the kind of person he or she will be in future. You have to observe and ask yourself the following questions impartially with regard to your future spouse.

- Does this person take any responsibility for his or her actions?
- Is this person honest and trustworthy?
- Is this person organized?
- Does he or she have goals in life?
- Is this person rude or arrogant?
- How does this person behave with people who are beneath him?
- Does this person display strange or abnormal behavior?
- Is this person an introvert or extrovert?
- Does this person ever show kindness to other people?
- Does this person get angry for no apparent reason?

Initially everyone tries to be on their best behavior when they are looking for a spouse. A person's true colors are only visible once you have met them often and have gotten to know the person well. Even your future mother-in-law can behave very nicely initially. It is easy to change your behavior while you are still young. As people get older they become set in their ways. They often continue their bad behavior or habits even when they know it hurts them as well as people around them.

When people are in love, they often ignore the bad behavior of their partners. Any sort of bad behavior not pointed out and corrected will only get worse with time and will cause friction in your relationship. If someone consistently displays bad behavior, then that is definitely a red flag.

Key tip: A person's behavior is very important. Your spouse should be a good person at heart.

Spending & Saving Habits

As this book has discussed before, money plays an important role in any relationship including marriage. Money is one of those things over which heated arguments can occur between spouses. My own parents (who have been married for over 30 years) still have arguments over money as my dad likes to keep spending and mom wants to save money.

It is preferred that at least one spouse should have financial literacy. It is surprising how so many well educated people are totally illiterate when it comes to finance, or are just unable to manage their finances properly.

There has to be understanding between you and your spouse once you start making important financial decisions such as buying a house, car, investing in stock market, insurance, mutual funds and running day to day expenses. On top of that you have to keep money aside for birthdays, festivals, shopping, vacations and any medical emergencies. If you have kids, the financial situation is even more complex. Now you can see for yourself why managing money properly is important.

While in the USA, I used to see some people at work driving brand new luxury cars even though their salary was relatively low. I once asked my co-worker how these people are able to afford such cars on their salary. He laughed and said that they are "30k millionaires". This is an American term used to describe someone who makes less money but spends lavishly often by maxing out their credit cards and taking out loans.

Key tip: While not apparent initially, financial compatibility is necessary if you want to avoid daily arguments in future.

Children

In the previous generation, life was less complicated. People just got married and had kids pretty soon. Having at least a couple of kids was considered to be a must. Many people lived in joint families or with in laws and most women too were housewives. Raising kids was not that difficult in such a household.

It might seem a bit farfetched to talk about children while looking for a spouse, but it is good to have at least a general discussion regarding the same. Some of the questions one should discuss are

- Do both of you want children or not? (many couples in developed countries remain childless by choice)
- If yes, then how many?
- Will one of you be able to stay home and take care of the child at least for the first couple of years?
- If not you, then are grandparents or other family members willing and able to take care of the child?
- Expenses of raising children (cost of schooling and college has gone up drastically in most major cities)

Most urban couples in India prefer to have only one or two children. Many urban women who are doing well in their jobs and careers often want to postpone marriage, and have their first child when into their 30s. This sounds like a good idea, but waiting too long to have children can often have serious health consequences for the woman and the child.

According to National Health Service (UK,) as women get older, both mothers and babies face an increased risk of pregnancy-related complications and health problems. [15] These are due to changes in the reproductive system and the increased likelihood of general health problems that come with age. These problems include:

- Greater difficulty in initially conceiving a child, with the personal and psychological difficulties that this can cause.
- Increased risk of complications for both mother and infant during pregnancy and delivery.
- Greater risk of general maternal health problems, such as high blood pressure, which can contribute to complications.
- Higher risk of miscarriage in women above the age of 35.
- Higher risk of having twins or triplets, which is itself associated with higher risk of complications.
- Increased chance of having a baby with a congenital abnormality, such as Down's syndrome.
- Increased risk of pre-eclampsia.
- Increased risk of complications during delivery, such as prolonged labor, need for assisted delivery or Caesarean section, or stillbirth.

A couple must be very secure in their marriage before they plan for kids. If there are frequent arguments and clashes then you should not plan to have children. Innocent children bear the brunt if a marriage falls apart.

Key tip: Kids are a huge responsibility. Make sure you and your spouse are prepared.

The Final - Compatibility & Happiness

It ultimately boils down to compatibility between two people and if they are genuinely happy with each other. No person is perfect but you should try and find someone who is perfect for you. While making marriage decisions many people think too much about the future. I feel that thinking too much about the future is useless as nobody knows what will happen 5 or 10 years from now.

Let me share a true story. On a cold snowy day in February 2011, I was supposed to drive along with a co-worker to a meeting with our company's clients in a neighboring city in Upstate New York. I had driven on that highway several times before and the travel time (one way) was about an hour. It was supposed to be a simple and routine trip. Little did I know that something would happen that would change my thinking forever.

I left the office parking lot with my co-worker in the morning and got on the Interstate-90. While driving, I noticed that it was very windy and the wind was blowing fine snow particles on to the interstate highway (imagine putting some talcum powder on a smooth floor and you put your foot on it). I continued to maintain a steady speed of about 65 miles per hour and stayed in the right lane so that the faster traffic could pass me in the left lane (passing lane).

Suddenly I encountered a rather large patch of this fine particle snow and without any warning I could feel the car skidding. As the car tires lost traction, the car did a 360 degree turn, crossed over into adjoining lane and slammed into the snow which was dumped on the side of the highway at over 60 miles an hour (over 95 kilometers per hour). All this happened in less than 5 seconds.

I somehow managed to open the door and got out of the car. A police SUV immediately appeared (without me even dialing 911) and stopped behind the car. The police officer turned on his flashing lights and blocked the lane so that no vehicle would hit us from behind (I was and still remain impressed by how efficiently and effectively various systems work in USA).

Fortunately, no one was killed or injured in what could have been a horrific accident. In USA, multiple vehicles accidents can happen, especially on highways. I and my co-worker pushed the car out of the snow and got back on the highway. We met the client and the rest of the day went normally.

I could have been killed in that accident, but somehow I survived without even suffering a single scratch. This set me thinking and I came to the conclusion that ultimately life has no guarantees. You might plan your life as much as you want, but you never know what plans life has for you. These are some of the life lessons I have learnt so far.

- You should do good actions but the outcome isn't in your hands.
- You should be able to balance courage with caution.
- Always trust your instinct. If you feel something is not right, then it probably isn't.
- You should believe in the power of good over evil.
- I admit that luck does play a role too but luck is something you should not blindly believe in.

Same thing can happen in a marriage. Uncertainty and risk are a part of life. You should try and live with that. There should be a mutual feeling that you are compatible and will be happy with each other. It is this feeling that will help you get over rough days. There will also be times when one of you will have to sacrifice something for your spouse and vice versa.

Key tip: There should be a deep mutual feeling of compatibility and happiness between both of you.

Miscellaneous Considerations

If you have indeed found someone and have decided to marry, then this chapter of the book discusses some of the things one must consider before actually getting married. You can ignore these things if they are not applicable to you.

Dowry

The dowry system is a curse on Indian society. The dowry system is the groom's parents asking for money or for other things such as gold, real estate, cars etc. from the girl's parents before or after marriage. I am totally against such practices. Many parents of girls do feel an obligation to give something to their daughter as she leaves their house forever and goes to her husband's house. Someone giving you something out of their own free will and without any sort of pressure is very different from asking for dowry.

It seems that even in this day and age, the dowry problem remains so severe that many profiles that I came across online had mentioned statements such as

"Dowry seekers please excuse."

"If you are expecting dowry in cash or kind, then please do not contact us."

"We are strictly against dowry."

Rates for dowry are decided based on the groom's caste, qualifications, professional position and income. If these parameters are high, then a very fat dowry is demanded. For wealthy people paying dowry is not a problem, but it is the middle class and the poor who bear the brunt.

One of the worst side-effects of the dowry system is the plummeting sex ratio in many states in India. Sex ratio is defined as the number of females per every thousand males. A girl child is viewed as a serious liability by many people; so serious that the moment a girl is born, parents have to start worrying about dowry. Thanks to proliferation of ultrasound machines, sex of the unborn child can be determined beforehand and sex selective abortions can be carried out.

The table below shows sex ratio in many states in India. This data has been collected from the website of the Office of the Registrar General and Census Commissioner, Ministry of Home Affairs, Government of India.[16] Extrapolating this data, one can come to the conclusion that there will be millions of more men than women of marriageable age in future. This means that many men might never find a wife because the women are simply not there!

These men can only blame the previous generations, thanks to societal preference for boys. This situation is similar to "Tragedy of the commons" often used in economics. Every family is trying to be selfish in choosing to have only a male child. But this selfishness repeated over millions of times means it is a societal and national loss. Your daughter is going to be some else's daughter in law and someone else's daughter will marry your son.

Statement 16

Sex ratio (female per 1000 male) at birth by residence, India and bigger States, 2010-2012

India and bigger States	Total	Rural	Urban
India	**908**	**909**	**904**
Andhra Pradesh	914	911	923
Assam	922	924	905
Bihar	909	911	891
Chhattisgarh	979	986	933
Delhi	884	892	882
Gujarat	909	922	885
Haryana	857	859	852
Himachal Pradesh	939	941	904
Jammu & Kashmir	895	895	894
Jharkhand	918	929	856
Karnataka	950	958	935
Kerala	966	963	979
Madhya Pradesh	921	920	927
Maharashtra	896	882	917
Odisha	948	952	921
Punjab	863	856	875
Rajasthan	893	900	868
Tamil Nadu	928	934	920
Uttar Pradesh	874	872	883
West Bengal	944	940	960

Source: Office of the Registrar General and Census Commissioner, Ministry of Home Affairs, Government of India

On the flip side some women also misuse the strong anti-dowry laws enacted by the government to protect them. One occasionally reads in the media the stories of how women file false cases against their husbands and in-laws destroying many lives in the process.

One possible suggestion is to use the services of a lawyer before marriage. A legal agreement can be drawn up which can clearly specify that no dowry was exchanged. If any gifts are exchanged voluntarily then that can be clearly specified. This can protect both parties in case any conflict arises in future.

Key tip: Do not pay any dowry in cash or kind. Refuse to marry if asked for dowry.

Wedding Expenses

Indian wedding often tends to be an elaborate affair from start to finish. Various communities have their own unique rituals. As Indian economy has boomed in the last few years, increasing number of people have been spending lavishly on weddings. An entire industry has grown to cater to every sort of whim or fancy you might have. Some examples of ostentatious display of wealth are

- Multi cuisine (North Indian, South Indian, snacks/chaat (pani puri, bhel puri etc.), Chinese, Mediterranean and so on). *If possible, please consider donating excess food to charity organizations or needy people.*
- Several sets of very expensive designer clothes. This is not just for the bride and the groom but for several family members too.

- Limousines or luxury cars to ferry the bride and the groom.
- Wedding themes. These can be very expensive and often serve no purpose other than show-off.

One of my friend's dad is a branch manager at a major public sector bank. My friend told me how his dad used to tell him that many people would take out huge loans for weddings. The loan money would usually be spent on all wedding related expenses including but not limited to buying gold jewelry and expensive clothes, the wedding and in some cases for honeymoon in expensive locations abroad. Honeymooning in India is considered to be boring and many people prefer to travel exotic locations abroad often on borrowed money!

Once someone in the community spends a certain amount of money, it sets a benchmark for many other people. This can and often does begin an arms race to keep spending more. Even within the same family, if parents spend a certain amount of money for the elder child, it sets expectations among younger kids that the same or even more money will be spent for them.

Since 2008 USA and many other countries around the world have been in the midst of severe recession. Many people have understood that they were very much less rich than they thought themselves to be. On a positive note it has ushered in much needed frugality in many things including weddings. Almost everyone I knew there told me that weddings in USA are solemnized in a simple church ceremony. I was definitely impressed by this as compared to the often elaborate and expensive ritual of an Indian wedding.

In late 2013, one of my American friends, whose elder brother was getting married, told me how his brother and future sister in law were trying to save costs on their upcoming wedding. My friend later told me how they were able to save at least a few thousand dollars by managing costs carefully and avoiding wasteful expenditure. The things they did were

- They designed the wedding invitation cards themselves and took print outs. These printouts were then mailed to friends and family.
- They did most of their shopping from good quality discount stores instead of buying designer labels. This alone saved them hundreds of dollars.
- No limousines to ferry the bride and the groom.
- The reception menu was simple and they limited the number of items. There was no

limitation on the amount of food each guest could eat.

- They did spend money on alcohol and the wedding cake.

The bride, groom and their families must decide on a realistic budget for the wedding from start to finish. Since so many different costs are involved, there is always a good probability that some of the costs will be more than initial estimates, so do keep 10 to 20% more than the budget. This is wise planning for any unexpected expenses too.

Always remember this simple fact that the success of your marriage does not depend on how much you spend on your wedding.

Key tip: Avoid extravagance on the wedding and spend within your means.

Household Responsibilities

My friends who did get married often got a rude shock for the first few months of their married lives. After marriage every aspect of your life does change. Based on my discussions with my married friends I realized that the following are some of the issues one could face once the honeymoon is over and the day to day reality sets in.

Living arrangements is one of the first issues that come up after marriage.

- Where will you be living? Many times a woman has to move to a different city and even a country based on where her husband is living.
- In many conservative households across the country, women are still expected to do everything from cooking to cleaning the house. Domestic help may or may not be available.
- If you are living with your in laws then they could have additional expectations.
- Dividing household responsibilities if the couple is living alone. Who will do what?

A few other things that often come up

- How much share does each person want to contribute to running the household? Are personal expenses separate from common expenses?
- Do you want a joint bank account or do you want to keep separate bank accounts?

Key tip: Have a brief discussion (if you prefer) on living arrangements and sharing of day to day responsibilities after marriage.

To the reader,

I hope that *Dating and Marriage Diaries in Urban India* will help you navigate the difficult and complicated journey of finding a good spouse and hopefully have a strong, happy and lasting marriage. Always remember marriage is not that piece of paper (marriage certificate) issued by the government, but it is the love, care, fidelity and commitment that you have towards each other. I wish you the very best.

All The Key Tips

1. Girls (and guys too!) should have a smiling and pleasing personality. It is important to invest in your own health and fitness.

2. Marrying someone living abroad carries substantial risk even in the best of times. If you choose to go down this path, then be extra careful and do it at your own risk.

3. Never marry for money. It's very rare to find a girl who is rich and is level headed.

4. The girl should be actively involved in the selection process and not parents or relatives.

5. If you indeed want to date/marry a divorcee then my advice is to wait at least 6 months to a year after the divorce has been legally granted. This may give them enough time to put their life back on track.

6. Freedom and responsibility go hand in hand. If you abuse your freedom and make poor choices

then you alone should bear the responsibility for the same.

7. Working hard is a good thing but at the same time you should relax and do fun activities that you enjoy.

8. Girls should learn to be more assertive, develop social skills and make their decisions themselves.

9. Do not accept or reject a person solely based on his or her caste.

10. Believing only in horoscope with complete disregard for all the other factors is a recipe for disaster.

11. While making a marriage decision, always remember a good job today is no guarantee of perpetual financial security.

12. Online matrimonial sites offer a good way to meet potential spouses; you should create a good profile and must be able to manage it properly.

13. Try to avoid using the services of marriage agents. Verify beforehand if you decide to use their services.

14. Do not agree to marry overweight or obese persons until they make a firm commitment to reduce their weight. Make sure they back their commitment with action.

15. The girl and the guy should undergo complete medical checkup before marriage.

16. Given all the health risks of smoking, this is a no brainer. Do not marry a smoker.

17. Make sure your future spouse does not drink alcohol in excess. Teetotalers are an even better option.

18. Anyone who uses drugs is a strict NO!

19. Be clear on what your expectations are with regard to age and height of your future spouse.

20. You should be comfortable with your spouse's dietary habits.

21. Do not hide anything about your past from your future spouse. You must be mentally, emotionally and physically ready for marriage.

22. If you are a homosexual then please do not ruin someone else's life by entering into a heterosexual marriage.

23. Educational attainment is a good (though not the only) thing to have in a future spouse.

24. Looks are important but one should not be obsessed about them. Maintaining good personal hygiene is very important. Bonus points for well-groomed persons.

25. Doing together the activities that you both enjoy is a good way to bond and be close to one another.

26. A person's behavior is very important. Your spouse should be a good person at heart.

27. While not apparent initially, financial compatibility is necessary if you want to avoid daily arguments in future.

28. Kids are a huge responsibility. Make sure you and your spouse are prepared.

29. There should be a deep mutual feeling of compatibility and happiness between both of you.

30. Do not pay any dowry in cash or kind. Refuse to marry if asked for dowry.

31. Avoid extravagance on the wedding and spend within your means.

32. Have a brief discussion (if you prefer) on living arrangements and sharing of day to day responsibilities after marriage.

References/Bibliography

1. Gary Ling and Stephanie McIntyre, China toddler fights fat in land of little emperors, *Reuters*, 1st April 2011, online at http://www.reuters.com/article/2011/04/01/us-china-obesity-idUSTRE7302QP20110401 (accessed 12th June 2015)

2. Kelly Clay, Why Microsoft's Layoff Is Much More Sweeping Than the 18,000 Cuts, *Forbes,* 20th July 2014, online at http://www.forbes.com/sites/kellyclay/2014/07/20/microsoft-layoffs-also-impact-thousands-of-contractors/ (accessed 15th June 2015)

3. India facing obesity epidemic: experts, *The Hindu*, 12th Oct 2007, online at http://www.thehindu.com/todays-paper/tp-national/tp-andhrapradesh/article1928668.ece (accessed 18th June 2015)

4. Calculate Your Body Mass Index, National Heart, Lung and Blood Institute, National Institutes of Health (USA), online at http://www.nhlbi.nih.

gov/health/educational/lose_wt/BMI/bmicalc.htm (accessed 18th June 2015)

5. What Are the Health Risks of Overweight and Obesity? National Heart, Lung and Blood Institute, National Institutes of Health (USA), online at http://www.nhlbi.nih.gov/health/health-topics/topics/obe/risks (accessed 18th June 2015)

6. U.S. National Library of Medicine, National Institutes of Health (USA), online at http://www.nlm.nih.gov/medlineplus/ency/article/002125.htm (accessed 19th June 2015)

7. Smokers in India increases to 11 crore people, *NDTV*, 8th January 2014, online at http://www.ndtv.com/india-news/smokers-in-india-increases-to-11-crore-people-547171 (accessed 21st June 2015)

8. What are the health risks of smoking? National Health Service (UK), online at http://www.nhs.uk/chq/Pages/2344.aspx?CategoryID=53 (accessed 21st June 2015)

9. Afshan Yasmeen, Gutka more harmful than other forms of tobacco, *The Hindu*, 1st June 2013, online at http://www.thehindu.com/news/national/karnataka/gutka-more-harmful-than-other-forms-of-tobacco/article4769653.ece (accessed 22nd June 2015)

10. Alcohol's Effects on the Body, National Institute on Alcohol Abuse and Alcoholism, National Institutes of Health (USA), online at http://www.niaaa.nih.gov/alcohol-health/alcohols-effects-body (accessed 23rd June 2015)

11. Traffic Safety Facts, Department of Transportation (USA), National Highway Traffic Safety Administration (NHTSA), December 2014, online at http://www-nrd.nhtsa.dot.gov/Pubs/812102.pdf (accessed 24th June 2015)

12. Mumbai Traffic Police, online at http://trafficpolicemumbai.maharashtra.gov.in/cloud/ocms.aspx?id=1001201# (accessed 24th June 2015)

13. Medical Consequences of Drug Abuse, National Institute on Drug Abuse, National Institutes of Health (USA), online at http://www.drugabuse.gov/related-topics/medical-consequences-drug-abuse (accessed 25th June 2015)

14. Division of Nutrition, Physical Activity and Obesity; Centers for Disease Control and Prevention, online at http://www.cdc.gov/nutrition/everyone/basics/protein.html (accessed 20th June 2015)

15. Poly Implant Prothèse, *Wikipedia*, online at https://en.wikipedia.org/wiki/Poly_Implant_Proth%C3%A8se (accessed 29th June 2015)

16. Chapter - 3 Estimates of Fertility Indicators, SRS Statistical Report 2012, Office of the Registrar General and Census Commissioner, Ministry of Home Affairs, Government of India, online at http://www.censusindia.gov.in/vital_statistics/SRS_Report_2012/10_Chap_3_2012.pdf (accessed on 30th June 2015)